D0981477

GHoST GiRL

Also by Amy Gerstler

The True Bride
Primitive Man
Past Lives (with Alexis Smith)
Bitter Angel
Nerve Storm
Crown of Weeds
Medicine

GHOST GIRL

AMY GERSTLER

PENGUIN POETS

PENGUIN BOOKS
Published by the Penguin Group
Penguin Group (USA) Inc., 375 Hudson Street,
New York, New York 10014, U.S.A.
Penguin Books Ltd, 80 Strand,
London WC2R 0RL, England
Penguin Books Australia Ltd, 250 Camberwell Road, Camberwell,
Victoria 3124, Australia
Penguin Books Canada Ltd, 10 Alcorn Avenue,
Toronto, Ontario, Canada M4V 3B2
Penguin Books India (P) Ltd, 11 Community Centre, Panchsheel Park,
New Delhi – 110 017, India
Penguin Books (N.Z.) Ltd, Cnr Rosedale and Airborne Roads, Albany,
Auckland, New Zealand
Penguin Books (South Africa) (Pty) Ltd, 24 Sturdee Avenue,
Rosebank, Johannesburg 2196, South Africa

Penguin Books Ltd, Registered Offices:
80 Strand, London WC2R 0RL, England

First published in Penguin Books 2004

10 9 8 7 6 5 4 3 2

Copyright © Amy Gerstler, 2004
All rights reserved

Page vii constitutes an extension of this copyright page.

LIBRARY OF CONGRESS CATALOGING-IN-PUBLICATION DATA

Gerstler, Amy.
    Ghost girl / Amy Gerstler.
        p.   cm. — (Penguin poets.)
    ISBN 0-14-200064-7
    I. Title.   II. Series.

    PS3557.E735G47 2004
    811'.54—dc22   2003060158

Printed in the United States of America
Set in Walbaum
Designed by Ginger Legato

Except in the United States of America, this book is sold subject to the condition that it shall not, by way of trade or otherwise, be lent, resold, hired out, or otherwise circulated without the publisher's prior consent in any form of binding or cover other than that in which it is published and without a similar condition including this condition being imposed on the subsequent purchaser.

The scanning, uploading, and distribution of this book via the Internet or via any other means without the permission of the publisher is illegal and punishable by law. Please purchase only authorized electronic editions and do not participate in or encourage electronic piracy of copyrighted materials. Your support of the author's rights is appreciated.

for Sidney and Miriam Gerstler

Acknowledgments

The author would like to thank the following people for their kind assistance:

Bernard Cooper, Dennis Cooper, Liam Rector, Judith Moore, David Lehman, Megan Williams, Paul Slovak, David Trinidad, Tony Cohan, Alexis Smith, Tom Knechtel, Brian Tucker, Jane Weinstock, Sue Greenberg, Dinah Mills. And most especially, Benjamin Weissman.

Many thanks to the Durfee Foundation whose Artists Award helped make it possible for the author to complete this book.

Poems in this manuscript were previous published in the following magazines, sometimes in slightly altered form:
Epoch, Fence, Tight, Slope, Luna, Lungful, Faultline, Bedwetter, Sycamore Review, American Poetry Review, Mall Punk, 5 AM, The New Yorker, Pool, The Cafe Review, Columbia Poetry Review, The Literary Review, Crowd, Green Mountain Review, Indiana Review, Washington Square, Mississippi Review, Poetry/Memoir/Story, and *Margie.*

The three poems "Buddha Sonnet 1–3" originally appeared in an artist's catalog for Darren Waterston published by St. Anne's Press. The poems "Swish" and "Witch Songs" were texts written for a collaboration with artist Alexis Smith entitled "The Sorcerer's Apprentice." Portions of those texts originally appeared as part of that installation, which began at the Miami Art Museum and traveled to the Museum of Contemporary Art, San Diego.

Contents

GHoST GiRL

Touring the Doll Hospital

Why so many senseless injuries? This one's glass teeth
knocked out. Eyes missing, or stuck open or closed.
Limbs torn away. Sawdust dribbles onto the floor
like an hourglass running out. Fingerless hands, noses
chipped or bitten off. Many are bald or burnt. Some,
we learn, are victims of torture or amateur surgery.
Do dolls invite abuse, with their dent-able heads,
those tight little painted-on or stitched-in grins?
Hurt me, big botched being, they whine in a dialect
only puritans and the frequently punished can hear.
*It's what I was born for. I know my tiny white pantaloons
and sheer underskirts incite violation.* Criers and crib-
wetters pursue us in dreams, till we wake sweat-
drenched but unrepentant, glad to have the order
by which we lord over them restored. Small soldiers
with no Geneva Conventions to protect them,
they endure gnawing, being drooled on, banishment
to attics. Stained by cough syrup, hot cocoa, and pee,
these "clean gallant souls" wear their wounds as martyrs'
garments. We owe them everything. How they suffer
for our sins, "splintered, bursted, crumbled . . ." Every
bed in the head replacement ward is occupied tonight.
Let's sit by the legless Queen doll's tiny wheelchair
and read to her awhile if she wishes it. In a faint
voice she requests a thimbleful of strong dark tea.

Falsetto

A guy with a heavenly singing voice like Al Green's
can make you believe he's being melted alive, liquified
by pure yearning. The result is a kind of bee-less sung
honey. The singer I'm listening to this hot summer noon—
Dean, or is it Gene—sounds like he's auditioning to be
female. No, it's more like he swallowed a woman whole,
without even mussing her lovely hair. Now their duets,
entwined laments, spill from his lips, reveries of what
each has embraced, squandered, fucked, drunk up.
His singing gives off a whiff of what we once called *sin*.
Then she slipped off her girdle, and we recognized
her as *blessing*, or maybe her kid sister, *bliss*. Jonah
in the whale's belly pleaded sweetly with god,
warbled a high-pitched SOS. Falsetto elected a nest
of tiny silver cobras who twist themselves into treble clefs
to represent it on paper. Those within earshot close
their eyes as the cries of bog men and ice maidens mating
rise from an abandoned amber mine. He who sings perfect
soprano like this, he who wields the orchid sword
cannot be resisted, at least until this record ends.

An Offer Received in This Morning's Mail:

(On misreading an ad for a set of CDs entitled *Beethoven's Complete Symphonies*.)

The Musical Heritage Society
invites you to accept
Beethoven's Complete Sympathies.
A full $80.00 value, yours for $49.95.
The brooding composer
of "Ode to Joy" now delighting
audiences in paradise nightly
knows your sorrows. Just look
at his furrowed brow, his thin
lipped grimace. Your sweaty
2 am writhings have touched
his great teutonic heart. Peering
invisibly over your shoulder
he reads those poems you scribble
on memo pads at the office,
containing lines like *o lethal blossom,*
I am your marionette forever,
and a compassionate smile trembles
at the corners of his formerly stern
mouth. (He'd be thrilled to set
your poems to music.) This immortal
master, gathered to the bosom
of his ancestors over a century ago,
has not forgotten those left behind
to endure gridlock and mind-ache,
wearily crosshatching the earth's surface
with our miseries, or belching complaints
into grimy skies, further besmirching
the firmament. But just how relevant

3

is Beethoven these days, you may ask.
Wouldn't the sympathies of a modern
composer provide a more up-to-date
form of solace? Well, process this info-byte,
21st century skeptic. A single lock
of Beethoven's hair fetched over $7,000
last week at auction. The hairs were then
divided into lots of two or three and resold
at astronomical prices. That's how significant
he remains today. Beethoven the great-hearted,
who used to sign letters *ever thine*,
the unhappiest of men, wants you
to know how deeply sorry he is
that you're having such a rough time.
Prone to illness, self-criticism
and squandered affections—
Ludwig (he'd like you to call him that,
if you'd do him the honor),
son of a drunk and a depressive,
was beaten, cheated, and eventually
went stone deaf. He too had to content
himself with clutching his beloved's
toothmarked yellow pencils
(as the tortured scrawls in his notebooks
show) to sketch out symphonies, concerti,
chamber music, etcetera—works
that still brim, as does your disconsolate
soul, with unquenched fire and brilliance.
Give Beethoven a chance to show

how much he cares. Easy financing
available. And remember:
a century in heaven has not calmed
the maestro's celebrated temper, so act now.
For god's sake don't make him wait.

The Slightly Perverse World of Music

Someone wakes you
by blowing gently on your eyes,
or tickling your chin with a handful of flowering grasses.
Remember the glassed-in greenhouse, the old fire station,
herds of black faced sheep?
Even strayed cows or a lone goat
may wander along a swath of fallow, unfenced mind
in search of tastier grazing from time to time.
Tonight, the reigning notes are sad and forlorn,
long lost octaves hung out to dry,
flashes of forgotten nights,
besotted, bawdy, sleepless,
and all too brief.

THE FETUS' CURIOUS MONOLOGUE

My tail was longer than my hindlegs
not so long ago. I remember the Flood
several Ice Ages   being covered with fur
chalk beds   trilobites   giant ferns
a scaley monstrosity crawling out of the sea
croaking *a great surprise awaits you*

Will I too grow fins? feelers? an elephant's trunk?
Cheerful to this hour, afloat in my private ocean,
I plan to make a grand entrance,

howling in molten dialect, *Even the sea's spooky depths*
shall not alarm me for I am already sunk!
The life of darting shadows, the deceptive surface
of the world—I shall see right through
to the seaweedy bottom. I will not be fooled!

The body's hinges itch.
Gill slits ventilated my neck
until yesterday.
A newfangled monster,
Now what will I breathe?

green lipped mussels
horseshoe crabs
coral and snails
waterworms

all sing of unalloyed joy and reciprocrated lust—
proof of progress, proof that evolution

is not just erosion, proof chiseled from limestone quarries
of womanly virtue (ageless patience, the warp and woof
of heredity's tireless loom),
    proof we do not really die
        when our brief terms expire

My pink lungs are mutated
swim bladders of fish.
A solitary wasp of consciousness
buzzes in my head while below,
the usual two room shack,
a bi-chambered heart is being constructed.

Someday I will have a scarlet hat and a ring,
perfect pitch,
a longing to be admonished.
Torn from the shores of immortality
I'm due to wash into the world soon,
wearing the face of a retired opera singer
mid-aria, famished and squalling.
I'm a festival of cells.
My blood's as rich as Christmas
punch. Was I a horse thief in another life?
A blasphemous priest? What were my crimes?
What have I done to deserve to be bottled up thus?

Fate

Reports of strange gatherings at the church in the pines
have been filtering in. It's said photogenic intellectuals
appear from time to time as mist in the kitchen. One groans,
   "Yes, I built the doomed ship and was promised I'll suffer for it.
   In lives to come I will know titanic miseries. This I have been:
   a hindrance and a snitch and a babysitter and a ranch hand.
   And a fry cook and a civilising influence and a whimperer.
   Catching wind of the near-death experiences of the little blind
   waif traveling to Africa made a believer of me. She cured
   my not-so-subliminal jitters. 'Picture me naked, if it helps
   quiet your mind,' she suggested, fingering pins jabbed
   into the small black cloth voodoo doll in her pocket.
   Now she belongs to the soil and the sky, proof of our puniness.
   When I lie my cleanest, most blameless self down in a bare,
   airless room, a warning voice, hers of course, jabbers
   gruff barracks talk. She says, 'You're all washed up, buddy,'
   'At last, my love, I'm here,' and 'Get dressed quick, for you
   too have been summoned.' So when I wake up smack dab
   in the middle of the night shouting the names of my fellow
   passengers, prisoners really, urging them to jump
   into the heaving sea, now you'll know why."

THE FLOATING WOMAN

Know, my dears, that gravity
is conditional. Its grip is no stranglehold.
Had my mother lived I could
have taught her this. I was nine
when she died clipping coupons
at the kitchen table on a sweltering day.
She wore only her slip, inside out, so you
could see the seams and mended hem.
A baseball game flickered on TV
with the sound off. I could hear small thuds
as figs from the tree in our yard fell and hit
the tin roof. I caught pneumonia
that summer and for months outslept
everyone, even the cat. Then Dad
crashed his beloved car (an ancient
pale green Mercedes with fins
and a mermaid hood ornament
he'd sawed off an old swim trophy
of mother's one inebriated evening).
When I got well I began to lie
in a big pile of eucalyptus leaves behind
the house and practice rising. With my
talents I could have toured the world
but I do not profit by travel.
I let a local magician think
it is all his doing, but in truth I float
under my own power. Sacrifice lightens,
voluntary or not. Loss rids us of ballast.
Then come the ascensions . . .

Witch Songs

Women really are diabolical.
Ask one, she'll admit it.
They're all witches under the skin.
Plotting, scheming, their recipes
need ingredients like graveyard
dust and possum teeth.
Those they have molested fear them.
They persist in begging
and become unpopular in their villages.
Witches are said to kiss beasts.
I say Kiss ye beasts while ye may.

One witch caused all the cupboards,
closets and drawers to spring open
in the house of a woman who'd denied
her food when she knocked,
starving and weak, at the kitchen door.
The witch put a toad in the woman's shoe
and

      Ha Ha

           next day she couldn't walk.

Riddle: what's the difference
between a recipe and a spell? Answer:
They're the same. Both have wicked intent.
The heart is reached through the stomach.
Your intestines are an undulating snake
she croons to through your flesh.
They hiss and spit and do her bidding.
Soon your other eager organs follow suit.

God gets jealous when eclipsed.
Use nought but a wooden spoon
to stir this brew. You who wish
to gain revenge or affix a curse
must find a tree your heart
selects as its own, branches
smooth as the limbs of a beloved
younger brother. This invitation
written in semen and ash—
can't we just reply in ink?

Scald and muddle some onions. Braise
a tourniquet. No, a tornado, I mean. Praise
the swollen, seedy tomato. Scold the shy
carrot, who thrusts his light underground.
Bring me the contents of your father's wallet.
Or you can substitute a folded hare's ear
if you find his pockets so difficult to pick,
you good for nothing, lazy girl!

You have bewitched me, my darling.
May I pet your horns, your tail?
You smell like autumn bonfires.
Afterward, the cradle rocked itself
for hours, but since she'd cured
the child's fever, we kept quiet
for a time. *Leave me be, you fainty cowards!*

She charmed me so completely I would
have done anything for her. Your soul
is imperiled by your ties to this woman.
At which speech the spirit did depart.
After this period of deep thought, the root
is sealed up in a jar with warm water
and set in a dark place for 8 days.
As she chants their names, one by one,
the winter stars appear.

Swish

A sweeping gesture, a sweeping defeat.
The hills sweep greenly down to the river.
Swept out to sea, swept off her feet.
The wind swept clay tiles from the roof
into the pool. Searchlights swept
the valley all night. Blight swept Europe.
The sweep of her hair made me weep
all afternoon, till I was tired and ill.
She made another silly, sweeping gesture
that knocked the peonies to the floor,
shattering grandma's vase into tiny,
teeth-sized pieces. Litter. Debris.
The sweep of a machine gun. Terrible
scenes that can't be swept from memory
so easily. He swept into the room,
blowing smoke rings, snickering
at some private *bon mot*. We swept
the election. Broad sweeps of jasmine
tremble at the forest's edge. Come lie down
with me on that rumpled shrub bed. The hem
of your nightdress will sweep the wet leaves.

The Oracle at Delphi, Reincarnated as a Contemporary Adolescent Girl

I'm high most of the time on hallucinogenic fumes.
Fumes pursue me, unfurling from the freezer
as I creak open its vault-like door to sneak ice cream.
Dizzying invisible gases leaked from my *hello kitty* backpack
all through elementary school. They seep from under
my bed at night like soporific fog. A species
of ether rose from the skins of boys I french
kissed at parties in junior high. (That's nonsense about
my needing to be a virgin to soothsay. Quite the contrary.)
Anyway, boys' male vapor gives me instructive whiffs
of what they're filled with: turbulent heroics, tinged
with an ancient hunt-and-gather tang. Back in Greece,
in that reeking temple, I was able to tell
men's fortunes just by the way they smelled.

The Pastry Chef's Daughter

His only child, I was my father's accomplice
in the kitchen. He taught me to skin nuts, poach
figs and plums, make cognac ice cream
and chestnut puree, to crystallize violets. I miss
his elegant cakes and soufflés, our breakfasts
together before dawn, flour whitening his curly
black hair prematurely. Mother succumbed
before I was two. So I never really knew
this pale slip of a girl I'd be shown in old,
darkening photos, a floppy bow in her hair
as though a butterfly had lighted there. Papa
began as a convent cook. His desserts, a kind
of heaven on earth, were so rich the nuns worried
his coconut meringue and peanut butter fudge
might be sinful. Later, Papa gave his pastries pious
names to put the nuns at ease. When he opened
his own bakery the names remained: Our Lady's
Crème Brûlée, Sermon on the Mount Whiskey
Raisin Cake, Holy Ghost Biscotti. Papa once
presented his nuns with a pumpkin mousse
Tower of Babel in a shallow lake of vanilla
crème anglaise, adorned with chocolate shavings.
What an offering. I'd like to believe all our efforts
in the world, however humble or exalted, are forms
of prayer, like Papa's worshipful, spirit-raising
pastries. Who's to say celestial insight can't ride
into the mind on a forkful of sour cherry pie?
Those who have kissed a thousand sugary mouths
or gloried in brioche glazed with apricot jam know

the tongue can serve as the soul's welcome mat.
Perhaps we often miss hints of salvation when it enters
us through the senses. A lick of lemon curd, a praline,
a chocolate leaf . . . crumbs of love and belief.

Fuck You Poem #45

Fuck you in slang and conventional English.
Fuck you in lost and neglected lingoes.
Fuck you hungry and sated; faded, pock marked and defaced.
Fuck you with orange rind, fennel and anchovy paste.
Fuck you with rosemary and thyme, and fried green olives on the side.
Fuck you humidly and icily.
Fuck you farsightedly and blindly.
Fuck you nude and draped in stolen finery.

Fuck you while cells divide wildly and birds trill.
Thank you for barring me from his bedside while he was ill.
Fuck you puce and chartreuse.
Fuck you postmodern and prehistoric.
Fuck you under the influence of opium, codeine, laudanum and paregoric.
Fuck every real and imagined country you fancied yourself princess of.
Fuck you on feast days and fast days, below and above.
Fuck you sleepless and shaking for nineteen nights running.
Fuck you ugly and fuck you stunning.

Fuck you shipwrecked on the barren island of your bed.
Fuck you marching in lockstep in the ranks of the dead.
Fuck you at low and high tide.
And fuck you astride
                    anyone who has the bad luck to fuck you, in dank hallways,
    bathrooms, or kitchens.
Fuck you in gasps and whispered benedictions.

And fuck these curses, however heartfelt and true,
that bind me, till I forgive you, to you.

Listen, Listen, Listen

Must you pray so loud? Is your god hard of hearing?

Each and every word should be pronounced in a manner that will ensure its purity of color and unmistakable identity.

Even though he was speaking through a medium, I'd recognize my dead boy's voice anywhere. He used his little nickname for me: *spittoonia.* It rhymes with *petunia.*

"At the sound of your voice/heaven opens its portals to me."

Coyotes congregate on the horizon, keening. *We greet the whitened bones of the eaten. We gnaw them down to mulch, to dust. Our duty is holy, holy, holy.* Elephants hit rumbling notes far below the threshold of human hearing, bridging vast distances.

It's said our crooning even reaches those entombed in coma.

The infant pickling in the jar of her womb picks up her mother's humming. Thus they vibrate in unison a long time before meeting face to face.

> *Anyone who faithfully follows the principles*
> *and practices given in this book will acquire*
> *a richer more resonant voice, and thus increase*
> *their power and influence in the world, to say*
> *nothing of their popularity and sex appeal.*

bleat grunt low cheep yelp trill hoot bay howl quack whicker snort yip ahem ladies and gentlemen . . .

All languages are beautiful when spoken or sung in resonant, well-modulated tones. Thus do qualms, psalms and lust-bitten lyrics pour out of your mouth and moisten the dry world.

That summer we had a contest to see who could make the most outlandish noises during sex but still not be overheard by the lumbering parents upstairs.

My thoughts do stutter, lisp and simper when it comes to you.

Boys and girls have vocal chords of about the same size until puberty. Then the voice box of the boys suddenly grows larger and their voices change. This shift has pillaged many a boy soprano's life.

Always attack a word with a loose breath and a wide-open throat.

Whisper the following distinctly nine times: *I uprooted the daffodils for sassing me back. She dreamed you kneeling. I write farcical odes based on the zodiac. He practices a toothless form of voodoo. Your genial deity is secretly a heel.*

Despite your unfortunate parentage I expect you to learn to perfect your consonants. Only then will you be accepted into polite society.

I realized something was wrong when the voice teacher forbid me to wear a bra to my lessons. Once he unzipped my mother's dress right in front of me. She just laughed and zipped it back up again.

Orpheus' severed head washed up on the shore of the island of Lesbos, still singing.

Humpback whales may sing for up to 20 hours nonstop.

It is not known why cats purr. Their production of this throbbing whir does not serve any discernable biological purpose.

How could I fall in love with his speaking voice, all gravel and nasally twang? It sounded like burnt potatoes being scraped off the bottom of a baking pan, or chiselers drilling in a marble quarry. Yet back then, nothing was as erotic as hearing him gruffly order a burger, or clear his throat. Ah, and his donkey guffaw . . .

Carefully pronounce the words *soft cloth*. Each vowel has its own savor and tang. Say *Icy diamonds suffice*. At least we can still warm and anoint each other with words when so much else has fallen away. Say *What glorious pork!* Say *hideous police machine*. Say *dubious human future*. Say *Prove he is in the tomb*.

We received a botched phone call from a ghost late last night. He could not make himself understood above the crackling static. It sounded like the room he was in was on fire. He seemed to be saying *My mental cutlery's grown dull, I have lost the knack of speech; the waters of pure thought have closed over me* . . . but that can't be right.

Put a cork in it, sister.

The doll insulted me in a barely audible voice. Her words seemed squeezed from her molded plastic head, like icing extruded from a pastry bag. She had a mouth like a pinhole and used surprisingly salty language for a toy. Then she hauled off and hit me with her small useless hand, its fingers fused, digits indistinctly articulated. It didn't hurt. In fact, I hardly felt the blow. Still, I threw her across the room to show her who was boss.

The kitchen drain gargles its aria . . .

Giraffes are silent. All that magnificent throat, the long purple tongue unfurling like a livid ribbon, and no voice at all.

Say, now that I have you on the horn . . .

There's a theory that some women who've been victims of sexual abuse as little girls have high squeaky voices as adults. This is because they remain "stuck" in the childish register corresponding to the age at which the abuse occurred. Could such a thing be true? Can vocal development be arrested at the moment of trauma? Do their voices halt and wait to confront the assailant in tones he or she will recognize?

In screaming or shouting all the muscles in the larynx are voluntarily contracted and tightened.

One of the autistic boys who attended the afternoon session could sing the words to dozens of LPs' worth of songs but could not speak. "Different parts of the brain are involved," the supervising psychologist told me.

You were such a wonderful singer. You seemed most glad of your life mid-song. I wish you could have bequeathed me your voice. I have a terrible, grating singing voice, and no sense of pitch. It's like tadpoles and algae being pureed in an electric blender. Still, I love to sing. Since you died I have this dreadful feeling sometimes when I warble to myself that you are listening and cringing.

If the eyes are the windows of the soul what is the voice? Its creaky drawbridge? Its dapper, garrulous ambassador? A smoky tasting moonshine it distills to inebriate unwitting listeners?

"Don't talk/put your head on my shoulder."

How can one successfully "put over" a song? Here are three simple hints.
1. Wear tight clothes.
2. Remember you are not really part of the frightful adult world.
3. Worship the listener.

As a teenager, Ella Fitzgerald, the "First Lady of Song," possessor of one of the most gorgeous voices ever heard, had actually wanted to become a dancer, like Earl "Snakehips" Tucker, whom she admired.

What does the bible say about the voice of the turtle? That it heralds the end of the world?

Buddha Sonnet I

Awake among sleepers, he knows
the hypnotist's loneliness. Robed in clusters
of bubbles, skull cup in his right hand,
he catches bitter milk that runs from
the world's wounds and drinks it down
quickly. Curled in fetal sleep inside one egg
among hundreds, a salamander hums as her cells
multiply. The buddha simply whistles along.
No surprise to find him in the garden tonight,
up to his wrists in wet earth, among pistils
and stamens, an intricate cloud pattern
draping his loins. In the sky, bruised colors
collide. Seeds disperse on the wind while
snails mate in mud from yesterday's rains.

Buddha Sonnet 2

Everlasting flower, wipe the frosting
off your lips and listen to me. Did you eat
that whole wedding cake all by yourself? You
cunning little thing. I hope you saved a sugar
rose for me. Your archaic smile has set me ablaze.
I can't contain myself any longer. I'll burst like
a mattress that's been used as a trampoline. I'll
erupt like your personal inferno, like the volcano
that buried Pompeii after its citizens ignored
years of rumbled warnings. Tonight the air's
full of murk, musk and strange strangled moans.
Say you'll be mine. I'll dip my fingers in the moon's
bright saliva and paint synagogue windows, or chaos'
names, like rings of kohl, around your riveting eyes.

Buddha Sonnet 3

He had so much dirt under his nails
I had to lay aside his rake and fuck him
right there, beside the zinnias he'd been
planting, our heads full of the scent
of turned earth and the worms'
choreography. Soil's made of death
mixed with perpetual foreplay, like a pond's
dark, teeming surface. If the buddha keeps
his back to you, seduce him. Kiss his rough
stone face, worn lips, calm nose. Make him
go five days without sleep, till his mind's
a bleary mess, till his thoughts are sticky beads
of moisture clinging to a rotting leaf, destined
to live again and again, despite its misgivings.

THE NEW DOG

I.

I'm intensely afraid of almost everything. Grocery bags, potted poinsettias, bunches of uprooted weeds wilting on a hot sidewalk, clothes hangers, deflated rubber balls, being looked in the eye, crutches, an overcoat tossed across the back of a chair *(everybody knows empty overcoats house ghosts)*, children, doorways, music, human hands and the newspaper rustling as my owner, in striped pajamas, drinks coffee and turns its pages. He wants to find out whether there'll be war in the mid-east this week. Afraid even of eating, if someone burps or clinks a glass with a fork, or if my owner turns the kitchen faucet on to wash his hands during my meal I go rigid with fear, my legs buckle, then I slink from the room. I pee copiously if my food bowl is placed on the floor before the other dogs'. I have to be served last or the natural order of things—in which every moment I am about to be sacrificed—*(have my heart ripped from my chest by the priest wielding his stone knife or get run out of the pack by snarling, snapping alphas)*—that most sacred hierarchy, that fated arrangement, the glue of the universe, will unstick. Then evolution will reverse itself, and life as we know it will subside entirely, until only the simplest animal forms remain—jellyish headless globs of cells, with only microscopic whips for legs and tails. Great swirling arms of gas will arm-wrestle for eons to win cosmic dominance. Starless, undifferentiated chaos will reign.

II.

I alone of my litter escaped a hell of beatings, neglect, and snuffling dumpsters for sustenance before this gullible man adopted me. Now my new owner would like me to walk nicely by his side on a leash (without cowering or pulling) and to lie down on a towel when he asks, regardless of whether he has a piece of bologna in his pocket or not. I'm growing fond of that optimistic young man in spite of myself. If only he would heed my warnings I'd pour out my thoughts to him: *When panic strikes you like a squall wind and disaster falls on you like a gale, when you are hunted and scorned, wisdom shouts aloud in the streets: What is consciousness? What is sensation? What is mind? What is pain? What about the sorrows of unwatered houseplants? What indoor cloudburst will slake their thirst? What of my litter brothers and sisters, dead at the hands of dirty two legged brutes? Who's the ghost in the universe behind its existence, necessary to everything that happens? Is it the pajama-clad man offering a strip of bacon in his frightening hand (who'll take me to the park to play ball if he ever gets dressed)? Is it his quiet, wet-eyed, egg-frying wife? Dear Lord, Is it me?*

The Days of the Week

form the spine of our lives. And like fraternal vertebrae,
theirs is an interlocking, unalphabetical procession—
a caravan of donkeys who chew ruminatively as they
file down a narrow mountainside trail, flicking
hairy tails to keep from being bitten by horseflies.
Generations of days like unruly school children line up
to audition for the annual Christmas play, poking
each other with gnawed yellow pencils. "Settle down!"
the teacher chides. "You'll never be cast as Jesus or Mary
if you keep behaving this way." *Soonday, Broomday,*
To You! Day, Whatever???day, Stirred Up Day,
Fried Mind Day, Stone Soul Zombie Day. We're given
seven Alpine huts 24 hours' journey apart. Carefully
secreted in each: firewood and flint, tallow candles,
dried apricots and sausage, a couple of chocolate bars,
wine in dusty green bottles. A holey blanket, an oil lamp,
and a stack of dogeared reading material. Freud's *The Ego*
and the Id with some pages missing, six issues of *Popular*
Zoology, cliff notes to *The Tempest,* sheet music
for seasonal drinking songs, *The Vegetarian Epicure,* and
a new translation of Lucretius' treatise *The Way Things Are.*

Poem for Bernard

*"It is in the power of every hand to destroy us, and we are beholden unto everyone we meet, he
doth not kill us."* —Sir Thomas Browne

We're down here in the basement
dodging bombs. As our loves
freckle with age we must adore
them more ferociously. Come winter
you kick back and ready your weapons

for spring. My next task was to get well.
Five million years ago, there were different
terrors. Saber toothed fears. Edgar Allen Poe
was terrified of being buried alive. Fear
is a civilising influence. It keeps us in line.

Fear of bacteria. Of our own murderous
kind. Of aliens superior to us in every
way who'll arrive any moment
and sensibly decide to clean house.
A terrible cry arises from the thick

of things. My begging bowl
runneth over. Heaven has been
relocated and we're not telling you
where. Not even a hint. I don't love
you anymore. What might it mean

to die a worthy death
and how much should one brood
about that ahead of time?
I was just trying to get back
to the boat alive. Let us lurch forward

or hellward. What an adorable form
of anarchy when the body outwits us.
I am a heretic in their eyes, so they
will kill us both and murder your children
if they find our hiding place. Despite

everything, I awoke full of praise
for you, as I do each morning.
Coughing constantly, I rinsed
my hands and ate some seeded crackers.
I thought about your face and prayed.

Watch

Yesterday, your tired wife and I
drove to the medical examiner's
to retrieve your personal effects.
She dropped me off at the front
entrance. The women at work
in that bland flat-roofed building
looked like secretaries at various
high schools you were principal
of over the last thirty years. The
back room was being remodeled,
so ideal placement of fax
machines and the shredder
were under discussion. An older
woman with dyed blonde hair
searched the property closet twice
for your watch. "It's here on the
computer," she said, shaking
her head, "but I can't locate it
on the premises." She phoned
the exam room to see if they still
had it "down there." Finally, on her
third trip to the closet, she found it.
I signed for the sealed, formaldehyde
smelling plastic bag, a form printed
on it in black ink. *Reason confiscated/
offense. Arresting officer/chain of custody.
Location where obtained.* The same form
for every crime, accident, fatality.
When I returned to the car, I found
your wife asleep at the wheel.

Not wanting to disturb her, I stood
and watched her awhile through
the rolled up window. What would
I give this waking minute, *my car
my house every book I ever owned,* trifles all,
to be able to kiss your brow and rouse
you now as if from a needed sleep?
I tore the bag open with my teeth.
It tasted awful. Inside, your everyday
watch with brown leather band, still ticking.

ON WANTING TO SEE GHOSTS

Ghosts only come to those who look for them. —Holeti

I.

The underaged medium:

I go about shuddering, but that shall not harm me. It's my way of tuning up. Sit down gently. These chairs suffer under our weight. Sounds bounce around in the dark room—throat clearings and a bubbly squeak, like an old man sucking his teeth. All things have derelict life in them: pearl button, dry leaf, linen handkerchief. I'm in such sympathy with the infinite, it will not leave me be. Prankster spirits yank my braids like my little sisters did. Mama, who I have not seen in months, owns nineteen bibles. If you're a real Christian, she says, dread can never digest you. Why do you appear so suddenly, spirit, even before I call you, as the table groans and stretches its stiff painful legs?

First female sitter:

Darling, must you look that way? Transparent and pale? The ghost trope. It's rather silly. Are you supposed to resemble the soul's silky lingerie? You swish like a fleeing woman's skirts, like the bedding of the restless. You've become even more effeminate in death, importing a whiff of millinery shops with your entrance, or of women's prison. You always were a disappointment as a man. Only that one night, my nightgown suddenly in shreds between your teeth, did you please me, and then, typically, you went too far. *(She laughs mirthlessly.)* I was making up stories for months to explain the contusions. The smell of the shirt factory fire still clings to you: smoldering bolts of broadcloth and corduroy; singed pincushions.

A male sitter:

I see and hear nothing. Nothing at all. Perhaps I am too old. This fretting and retching, going bug-eyed and treble-voiced seems the business of women. I want a cigar.

Second female sitter:
Poor medium. Just a wisp of a girl, flat chested and angry. She doesn't look
well. Cries for bicarbonate. Why does she have to be naked during the séance?
I wonder how well her keepers are feeding her. And what's that stuff erupting
from her mouth now? Wadded up wedding veil? Celestial drool? One of
heaven's tiny geysers? Why did you make her say, "Paradise is still liquid and
unorganized?" Surely that can't be true. What makes me return to this house,
night after night, to hear this little girl wail? I'm a luckless gambler,
inscribing my most truant desires on you.

II.

PRINCIPLES OF THE NATIONAL SPIRITUALISM ASSOCIATION
AND AFFILIATED ORGANIZATIONS:

—We believe in Infinite Intelligence.
—We affirm that the existence and personal identity of the individual
continue after the change called death.
—We affirm that communication with the so-called dead is a fact,
scientifically proved by the phenomena of Spiritualism.
—We affirm that the gateway to reformation is never closed against any
human or soul here or hereafter.

Only mediums who have been *investigated* and found *conscientious* and
reliable may advertise in these pages.

III.

could you quit wavering, hold still a minute?
oh I'm just pretending. I strain my eyes till they smart
for stains or rips in the air, and see nothing.
she'll never return to me. I am alone.

Faint as shame at the age of consent, ghosts are fond of silver. Gold angers them, though. The little medium's keepers took her gold earrings away, claiming they caused spiritual static.

IV.

The mutability of mutable things itself gives them their potential to receive all those forms into which mutable things can be changed. And what is this mutability? A soul? A body? The form of a soul or of a body? No; I would call it "a nothing-something" or "an is-that-is not," if such expressions were allowed.
—St. Augustine

Not yet had I begun to pour out my groans to you . . .

V.

I have it on good authority: the spirit realm is run by governments not unlike those of the Caesars of Rome.

Third female sitter:

One cannot say whether you walk or glide, form without form, shape without shape, exhausted footsoldier, misty bicyclist, animated splash of seltzer borne on breezes that smell of frying pork chops and just dug up onion. Tonight only your lips are visible. Are you too tired to materialize entirely? Did you approve of where your ashes were scattered? We hoped you'd think Convict Lake was an amusing place name, and that perversely, you'd find a kind of peace there. Its shallows are fringed with algae. In summer, the water's four shades of green. My new husband and I have a cabin up there. You didn't reply to any of my questions tonight, dear, but when I stood up from the séance table, there were your familiar teethmarks in my thigh.

Circus Poster

NOW *for a limited time only:*

SEE fleas recreate famous paintings!

HEAR heretics converse with birds that speak Greek!

TASTE the tears of our blubbering giant: guaranteed a gallon each!

SNIFF the wrists and earlobes of aromatic Prince Mandrake
from the mysterious East!

TOUCH the shuddering flesh of the famous Arkansas Fat Boy as he waltzes
you around his tent!

MARVEL as a turnip with beastly features lectures on vegetarianism!!

MARRY rich eligible lizards with felony arrest records!!

FEEL YOURSELF RIVETED TO THE SPOT as Fritz the Wonder Dog
performs bloodless surgery on your children!

SHIVER WITH DELIGHT while our grove of enchanted oak trees reads
your mind and makes public your innermost desires!

SWAY IN TIME to the tune stylings of Chilean sea snails who croon sweetly
while spelling out song lyrics in their glistening spittle!!

WIN A KISS from the beautiful lesbian mermaid!!!

. . . visit the world not as you believe it to be but as you have wrenchingly dreamed it . . . hairy infants, the easily fleeced, the sheepish, the greasy, rosy cheeked gymnasts with frilly little panties showing, wax figures of noted albinos missing digits, the devilish, the shipwrecked, the miserable, gladiators & ambulance chasers, quick-change artists & half-eaten gingerbread men: . . . IN SHORT every critter or crackpot will receive our warmest *Circus of Perversity* WELCOME!!! Admission: six shillings. Free admittance to all who submit to the Fat Boy's advances or permit the Electric Girl to frisk them——(the procedure often takes her several days.) Free lifetime pass to anyone who catches ME, your prodigiously endowed ringmaster with his sequinned trousers down.

COME ONE, COME ALL!!!!!

Pastoral Opera Synopsis

As the curtain rises, a tiny, unassuming weed
sings a haunting song: *Alas, My Seedpods Are
Lost to the Wind.* A sputtering lamp is about
to go out as a cattle breeder sits on his milking
stool in the barn inhaling the evening's cool air,
thumbing through a catalog depicting various
bulls. He's looking for a mate for Vanilla,
his favorite heifer, and they croon a charming
duet, *O Fragrant Hay.* Outside, destruction
of the farmer's crops by locusts is averted
as Monarch butterflies swarm and lead their
fellow insects to new feeding grounds: *Chirp on,
Winged Comrades!* Wild violets at the pasture's
edge tempt the lowing cows, whose bells
clanks as they amble home, to nibble their tender
leaves, paying gracious homage to the food chain:
By Our Aid the Stars are Weighed. All life forms
join in rousing chorus as the curtain descends.

White Blindfold

When I play it all back in my head, I recall only the joys of those hopeful decades. How good the grub was back then! How gently we bandaged the horses' eyes in order to lead them to safety after our barn was torched by the authorities. When the Dairy Fair judges declared the mold that gives our cheese its unique bite a kissing cousin to penicillin, doctors began to prescribe our homemade Brie for a wide variety of common ailments, from rheumatism to whooping cough.

In those days it seemed our good luck would never run dry. Then after the parade, after Taffy won an almond torte at the cakewalk, she was crowned Miss Sour Cream. Oh proud and grateful hour! During her coronation a spotted calf poked its head out from under her skirts, a bottle-fed orphan bawling for its mother. Next day the air smelled like chicken potpie and for once, my pocket didn't get picked. The high school marching band practiced for eight or nine hours straight, so folks who met in the streets found themselves hugging to music, whether they knew each other or not, a practice eventually called "dancing," which still persists today.

THE OGRE'S TURBULENT ADOLESCENCE

His hair hangs to his waist, uncombed,
clotted with dirt. Ladybugs and fire beetles
traffic his scalp. He chews tree roots,
keeps an ox as a lapdog, wears a python
for his watchband, and slobbers when he smiles,
which is oh so rarely, as it makes his face ache.
Listen, my darling little bone meal casserole, we're not
constructed for mirth, his mother patiently explains
several times each week. He writes in his diary:

> *I want a life of prayer.*
> *Why must I be this big?*
> *My body feels cumbersome*
> *and unholy, and I smell*
> *like the tar pits at high noon,*
> *sucking on the tusks of mammoths*
> *they've swallowed.*

On Sundays he dispenses treasure among the elves,
who he fears are not really his friends. Here's a photo
of the young ogre having a tantrum with the rope
from his yo-yo wrapped around his neck. Now how
did that happen? Here he is tearing up hymnals
and eating them, collecting giant bats for his menagerie,
blanching local foliage with his swampy breath that reeks
of a brown digestive drink called *fernet branca*,
popular among grumpy dyspeptic monsters.
Here he sits reading aloud from volume one
of *The History of the Pitiable* in a voice full of snuffles
and honks, mumbling on till cockcrow. Now he sobs,

now he sings. Now he gives voice to lingering
doubts about the longevity of the soul.
Now he discovers a pile of collapsed stone walls
incised with faint inscriptions he can read only by feel.
Light radiates from his fingertips (the size
of manhole covers) as he deciphers fragments
of advice and farewell notes from us, his ancestors,
a race of tiny insignificant beings, authors of our own
extinction. We observe his sufferings ever more
tenderly as we peer down at our lumbering cousin
over heaven's jagged and forbidding rim.

Domestic

Where's the wisdom in erasing a loved one's mess,
so akin to his signature? Your honor, I only meant
to strew the immaculate in his wake. To wipe the path
ahead and behind reasonably clean. Futile, yes,
but weren't such gestures essential to love's discipline
once upon a time? Daily, I harvested dropped fruit peels
and socks. I chased him through life with dustpan
and broom, smoothed his body dents from the bed,
soothed the mud tramped floors. Did I sin in this?
Better to leave the habitat sweetly reeking of him
than to spend years scrubbing up evidence of his existence.
Archaeologists centuries hence may marvel at such relics:
his mustard stained napkins, toothpicks chewed
to splinters. Never let it be said that in my zeal
to clean I robbed the future's museums. Who
am I to call what flies to either side of the trail
he blazes—half-read magazines, cups of scummed
over coffee and mashed out cigarettes—*dirt?*

Swans

A family of swans glides silently by,
their bills the reddish orange of flames
or some unwanted declaration.
Since I can't have you, I proposition
sentient beings outside my species.
Even the trees refuse me.
Why won't my mind be quiet?
Last night I dreamed you told me *no* again.
You scrawled FORGET IT on the clouded
mirror as I took a long, hot shower.
You were naked too, except for a thick pink
towel wrapped around your waist. Politely
you handed me a blue towel. Billowing steam
hid me like a chorus of Jewish aunts
at a ritual bath back in the old country.
Why do these longings persist? The two
adult swans steer closer to shore.
They nip at clumps of beard-like algae.
Their cygnets, the color of ash,
are quite shy. You can tell the male
by his flapping and honking. I sit on this dock
half the day, as though hatching an egg,
reading Daniel Defoe's history of pirates,
in which buccaneers brag and proselytize:
crying up a Pyrate's life to be the only one
for any man of spirit. About two in the afternoon
a guy without pistols or cutlass comes
to collect his bucket of bloody
fish caught the day before, stashed
in his moored boat. He tells me it's OK

if I sit there. Smiling, annoyed, I think,
what's it to you, buddy? Later I learn it's his dock,
his field of tall grass and Queen Anne's lace
I trudged through to get here,
so I've been tresspassing all day.
The male swan berates me: *Little fool,*
don't be so free with your love. I dangle my legs
over the oily bay. Globular rainbows
separate and unite on the surface
of the water. These trees can neither run
nor trudge, yet they flower and flower.

DENIAL

Don't think I spend my nights brooding
about your
freckled lips, smeared with fig jam.
Or your velvety
ear lobes. The way they taste of sea salt
and celery
never occupies my mind for hours at a time.
I've more chaste
things to meditate on, like the raft my son is roping
together down
by the lake, and whether it's even remotely seaworthy.
I am not
thinking about the biblical gardens of your armpits,
your slighty lemony
smell, the three white hairs sprouting from your right
eyebrow,
the coming storm in all its voluptuous glory.
I am merely
sitting on this itchy patch of beach grass, watching geese
land on sandbars,
recalling last night's dream, in which P.F. demanded
I write
a poem entitled "The History of English Lettuces."
This isn't it.

What the Body Wants

Not temperance or etiquette, but heavy petting.
Not modesty, but the sweaty *chase me* games
of childhood. Not renunciation, but chocolate
custard, served in mother's chipped pink ceramic
custard cups. Not bones, but the marinated all day
meat. Not pious missionary safaris, embarked on
limping and soul-injured in monsoon season.
No cautionary fore-glimpse of its burial place,
the trees waiting, patient and starved for nitrogen
in their secluded grove. The body, undaunted
scholar of its own encyclopedia of greeds,
craves a front row seat for the new satyr play,
lusts after the happy sacraments of black
cashmere sweaters midwinter, big dinners
with plenty of bread to sop up the gravy,
and long nights of athletic sex that leave it giddy
and winded, hallucinating dime-sized fireworks,
gasping that it can't continue, it'll expire
on the spot. Then a blessed second wind blows
in out of nowhere, followed by more naked
horseplay, racing thoughts, confessions whispered
into the darkened grate of another body's hazy face.
Soon absolution ensues, and a little late stargazing,
as the body teeters on the cusp of sleep. Next morning,
the whining, ungrateful mind arises unconsoled,
and the body must begin its cajoling all over again.

Bar Aubade

Tell me, tranquil objects surrounding
this pair as they sleep: you sheets, clock,
clothes lying in heaps on the unswept floor—
for example his shirt and her crumpled
stockings, co-mingling—surely it can't
yet be brisk, bittersweet day(?) Aren't light
and parting still far off, hiding behind
that crazy-assed purple horizon who
grumbles under his breath? Let's hope
that burgeoning, unearthly glow
is the blinking neon of a distant speakeasy,
wherein those destined to save themselves
by timely flight abroad meet to bid
each other adieu on the coast of a beloved
but deeply insecure homeland. The ashtrays
in this bar are always full. Our glasses are nearly
dry. A final fiery sip. OK. Time to go. Dawn's
the color of honey daubed on skin to promote
wound healing, or drizzled across the belly
in foreplay. Home is where you are fed
and adored. Hand me my crutches, dear.
We may yet escape the impending. I change
the bedding around here, so I know a thing
or two about who's in league with who,
and whose frail hopes are pinned upon whom.

ODE TO TOAST

"When you were alive 'Twas your favorite food . . ."

Lucky, lucky tongue, rejoice in toast's crisper,
toughened up crumb. The once limp slice stands up
to honey, mustard, blackberry jam, or pastrami piled
high, its folds like those of a Roman's toga. Amber
grain endured a second trial by fire. Toast is bread
twice baked, crustily double blessed, like the warrior
who twice escaped death at his enemies' hands
and survived into peace-time, not just unharmed
but husky, hardy and tanned by the sun, his grateful
faith intact. A blacksmith by trade he takes grave joy
in forging a plowshare from his sword. Toast's tooth-
some crunch echoes the sandpaper scrape
of a kiss from he of the unshaven cheek,
a kiss that turns my knees to melted butter.

ODE TO SEMEN

Whiteish brine, spooners' gruel,
mortality's nectar, potent drool,
foam on oceans
where our ancestors first
bubbled up (that vast soup
we'll one day
be stirred back into). . . .
O gluey sequel
to kisses and licks,
the loins' shy outcry,
blurt of melted pearl
leaked into hungry mouths
or between splayed legs
in a dim, curtained room,
while far off, down the hall,
in the kitchen's overlit,
crumb-littered domain,
ham is sliced,
potatoes are peeled,
and, emitting pungent milk,
minced onions
begin to sizzle . . .

(Poem That Spills Off the Page)

A List of Answers to the Question:

"And what, pray tell, were you wearing?"

Satyr horns.

Sackcloth and ashes.

My heart on my sleeve.

My spleen on my garter.

A crown of pink cactus flowers.

A grin the first rain washed away.

A cape made of a huge potato pancake.

His nectarine pit collection, strung as a necklace.

A clamshell bodice and a cockatoo on my shoulder.

Skirts stained by hors d'oeuvres and insincere platitudes.

A surly Marxist's tight-lipped rendition of lamentable events.

This hand-lettered sandwich sign which reads: *pardon my striving*.

A barrel of laughs, held up by suspenders, meant to conceal a leaky libido.

Layers of glacial lace and the last gasp of daylight. Jaguar pelts. Cosmic abundance.

My hair done up in the Spanish manner. A lilypad hat. The feel of your long absent hand

A Blessing and a Curse

(Spoken by a twelve-year-old girl wearing a paper crown. She addresses her younger brother.)

So far in this life, you've done me no harm. But in past incarnations your crimes against me were numerous and abominable. As punishment, you must spend a goodly portion of this existence making it up to me, or be reincarnated as a Beaded Gecko in the Gobi Desert next time around. I expect the first in a series of well-thought-out presents to begin arriving the day after tomorrow. I'll tell you when you can stop. And they better be nicely wrapped, too. You know what colors I like. Woe unto you if your offerings do not delight me to the wellsprings of my being. We shall both be exhausted before your forced worship of me runs its course. No one understands my rituals. You will study them and explain my winter injuries to our childlike followers, whose guileless, manic antics I alone was born to atone for. You'll trace ancient diagrams in the sand so they'll understand why my breath smells mostly like ammonia, why my halo of curls undulates like balletic water-worms at play, and why my future melon-like (but at this point in time still theoretical) breasts may be drunk from only on feast days or after a total eclipse. Don't make faces at me! Hold perfectly still while I anoint your sweaty, freckled forehead with this stripe of sacred paste, made from Brylcreem, gutter mud and catbox gravel. Kneel down right now and let me smear it on, before mother calls us in to wash our hands for lunch.

A Widow

Two Weeks Have Gone By, And

the dogs no longer sprawl on the family room
sofa, staring at the hall door in patient expectation
he'll stroll out of his bedroom and growl,
You two critters, get down off the couch! She donates
his clothes to charity, "so someone can get good use
out of them." Sunday, she makes jam, so the flats
of strawberries from Farmer's Market don't go
to waste. Floral tributes wilt in every room, mostly
stargazer lilies. She cancels his credit cards, driver's
license, car insurance, membership in the Discount
Buyers Club of America and The Mystery Book Guild.
Identity theft is a problem these days and the dead are prime
targets. Be sure to inform all creditors, banks, anyone with
whom the deceased did business. His colleagues drop by,
bearing more lilies and Danish lace cookies.
Some weep in disbelief, and she comforts them.

Free Ice Cream

Sixteen phone calls later there are still so many people
to break the news to. His barber, who cries;
their accountant, so sick his voice has thinned
to a gassy rasp. No quick, merciful end for that man.
He lingers another month. Then there's the ice cream
store girl who remembered the husband always wanted
rocky road, and scooped it without being asked.
She gives the widow and her daughter free ice cream.

Under The Rug

Oh, what a treasure hunt! Where did he hide
the deed to the house, his will, the health insurance
forms, the plastic trash bags—the big kind that tie
at the neck—the hedge clippers, the opera
tickets? His blood is expunged from the hall
rug where he fell, hitting his head after his heart
seized. Now there's not even a bleached spot.
When the widow told the cleaning lady that he'd
passed away, she insisted on staying to do her day's
work. She put in five hours vacuuming and crying,
dusting and sniffling, crying and ironing.

Nightlife

In dreams she relives his sudden, unexpected death
at a more graceful pace. He grows sick and dies
gradually, reasonably in these dreams, propped
on white pillows. She feeds him. They talk and talk.
Nothing's abrupt. All proceeds as languidly as water
ballet. Everyone behaves just beautifully. This second,
slower take on his death is so soothing, like a play
where actors take time with their lines, making
the most of their moment to step forward and address
the audience. Nothing in these dreams is drawn
from real life. In them, she never comes home after
dropping the dogs off to be groomed to find him
napping at noon (unusual, but not unheard of).
There's no jolt when she settles a quilt over him
and kisses his forehead, no bolt of fear as what touches
her lips, once his brow, is now a cold vacant dome.

Flocks of Birds

A troop of quail begins to visit her. A male
and his harem. She rigs a birdbath for them
in the backyard, hangs feeders and fills them
with peanuts and seed, watches birds
and squirrels through the dining room
picture windows as she drinks coffee.
She cuts her long hair. Her first shearing
in forty years. She looks younger, friends tell her.
The husky whines to be let out to chase quail.
I have a lot to live for she informs her daughters,
a statement she find strangely true.

Late Night Radio

Since his death she sleeps with his old radio
pressed against her ear—the transistor he'd
listen to with an earplug while patrolling the quad
at lunch, checking boys' restrooms for smokers.
All through the appalling, shapeless night, emphatic
voices prattle and buzz. They argue politics,
monogamy; urge her to texture-coat her home
or consider laser eye surgery; discuss fundamentalism,
and whether the Washington area sniper is a terrorist
or simply another deranged citizen. Blessed be
the radio with its chorus of vigilant souls who refuse
to let silence engulf our widow, and so, in
their own way, practice a doctrine of constant
love. Cajoled all night, she's never truly
    alone.

Ribs

She returns to food only slowly. At first she gags
down a few ounces of soup at her daughter's
insistence. As the days pass, her enjoyment
in eating gradually reawakens, like sensation
prickling back into a sleeping limb. Tonight
our widow is having pork ribs, slathered
in hot sauce made from chiles, catsup, cloves
and honey. As she eats, the dogs under the table
nuzzle her legs. The word "marrow" is stuck
in her head. It keeps repeating like the chorus
of a song, in time to her chewing. *You
were my plasma, sugarpie, my branching capillaries.
Baby, sweet baby, you were my marrow.*

MIRIAM

"And his sister stood afar off, to wit what would be done to him." —Exodus 2:4

She watches her brother float slowly downriver.
The water glows in spots like polished copper.
Moses sleeps in a reed basket, sealed with duck
grease and pitch. King of his own woven island,
he bobs gently away. She can't see his soft
mussed hair that never quite dries, his raw pink
upper lip. She absolutely refuses to bid him
goodbye. Sunrise makes her scalp prickle.
Dawn's her favorite time of day. The sky's
turning lavender five degrees at a time. This baby
loves daybreak, too. She reads him so easily.
His spirit, its weird infant flickerings, makes perfect
sense to her. She writes the baby's name on the river's
·surface, breaking its skin with practiced finger flicks.
Should she whisk her brother off to a cave and raise
him there? How dangerous can a baby be?
Sickly at first, his raspy cough made it tricky
to keep him hidden. He, too, loves donkey
bells, the burbling of doves. His face
crumples with joy when he catches a glimpse
of her. No one else has ever seemed that happy
to see her. The riverbank's oozy. Muck fills
her sandals. Her shift's clingy and smudged.
Thick foam, like cream on beer, collects around
clumped cattails. When she left on her mission
this morning, in utter darkness, her father hid
his head and wouldn't speak. Adults are such idiots.
No sane person sets an infant adrift. She winds
her braids so tightly around one hand her fingers
buzz. Bugs skim the river. Frogs burp. She yanks

off her filthy dress and drapes it over a patch
of reeds. She'll wade in and save him. When
he's older, she'll teach him to repeat: *I have
the prettiest sister in this village.* Hip deep in cloudy
water she sees a small crowd approaching.
Dressed in white, they're bearing someone
on a curtained litter, waving green palm fans.
So this is the future. You relinquish what you love,
offer it up, an unwilling gift. Her thoughts sputter.
*Separate. Unite. Separate. Unite. Death is an interim
state. A dead bough is a snake if that's what god
wants.* She feels light-headed and queasy. *Who is
that baby in the water I thought was my brother?*
A voice in and outside her, like jackals laughing,
or the horrible sucking of famished water
answers. *He is rash and tongueless. He is dust.
He is nothing. He is entry and exit, a radiant red
sky, a great vacancy, beloved and indestructible.*

Hʏмп ᴛo ᴛʜᴇ Пᴇᴄᴋ

Tamed by starched collars or looped by the noose,
all hail the stem that holds up the frail cranial buttercup.
The neck throbs with dread of the guillotine's kiss, while
the silly, bracelet-craving wrists chafe in their handcuffs.
Your one and only neck, home to glottis, tonsils,
and many other highly specialized pieces of meat,
is covered with stubble. Three mornings ago, undeserving
sinner though she is, yours truly got to watch you shave
in the bath. Soap matted your chest hair. A clouded
hand mirror reflected a piece of your cheek. Vapor
rose all around like spirit-infested mist in some fabled
rainforest. The throat is a road. Speech is its pilgrim.
Something pulses visibly in your neck as the words
hand me a towel flower from your mouth.

In the Aspirin Orchard

O analgesia trees! How your powdery
fruit soothes. Ancient tasting tablets
chalky as fossils dissolve on our tongues,

tame our pains. Wearing relief's
crown of flowers, sex re-enters
the room, uninvited, shy—

disguised as religion, robed in blessed
caresses that address every last malady.
Reckoned rightly, all suffices.

Misgivings licked clean, I abandoned
my love under a budding aspirin tree.
He was singing the chorus

of *Let's Pretend it's Snowing.*
He had a sleeping disease,
and often nodded off while

I was talking. Our treasure's
buried in clay pots where I first
nursed tender aspirin saplings

into bloom. I haven't the heart
to dig it up. Years have passed.
Our orchard prospered and spread.

Now hired pickers fill linen
aprons with harvests of dusty pills.
Like crumbs of asteroid

or hailstones, clusters
of ripening aspirins hang,
tiny alluring lanterns,

blurrily aglow. The merest sight
of them palely burns aches away.
Darling, do I hear the whining

of distant violins?
Let us kneel, for the age
of fevers is upon us.

"Touring the Doll Hospital" has some lines collaged into it from Walt Whitman's letters written while he was nursing wounded soldiers during the Civil War. The quotes appear in quotation marks in the poem. Two images at the end of the poem are also drawn from those letters, in which Whitman says of one injured soldier, "I do what I can for him . . . sit near him for hours if he wishes it," and of another, "He expressed a great desire for good strong tea."

In "Witch Songs," the line "They're all witches under the skin" is a slightly altered version of a line Bugs Bunny says at the end of a cartoon.

In "Listen, Listen, Listen" the line "At the sound of your voice/heaven opens its portals to me" is from a Rogers and Hart song. That poem contains three or four reworked lines from *The Human Voice: A Concise Manual on Training the Speaking and Singing Voice* by Franklin D. Lawson, Harper & Bros., 1944.

"The New Dog" contains some lines and language, in slightly altered form, from the Old Testament, Proverbs 1:23 and 1:27.

"In the Aspirin Orchard" contains an inversion of the poet Christina Rossetti's line: "all suffices reckoned rightly."

Amy Gerstler is a writer of poetry, nonfiction, and journalism who lives in Los Angeles. Her previous eleven books include *Medicine*, *Crown of Weeds*, which won a California Book Award, *Nerve Storm*, and *Bitter Angel*, which won the National Book Critics Circle Award. Her poems have appeared in a variety of magazines and anthologies, including *The New Yorker*, *The Paris Review*, *American Poetry Review*, and several volumes of *Best American Poetry* and *The Norton Anthology of Postmodern American Poetry*, and her journalism and art criticism have appeared in *Artforum*, *The Village Voice*, *Los Angeles Magazine*, *Los Angeles Times*, *Art and Antiques*, and numerous other publications. She teaches in the graduate fine arts department at Art Center, College of Design, in Pasadena, California, and is a member of the core faculty of the Master's program in critical writing there. She is a member of the core faculty of the Bennington Writing Seminars MFA program at Bennington College in Vermont, and has taught writing and/or art at the California Institute of the Arts, Cal Tech, the University of California at Irvine, the University of Southern California, and elsewhere.

TED BERRIGAN
Selected Poems
The Sonnets

PHILIP BOOTH
Lifelines

JIM CARROLL
Fear of Dreaming
Void of Course

BARBARA CULLY
Desire Reclining

CARL DENNIS
New and Selected Poems
*   1974–2004*
Practical Gods

DIANE DI PRIMA
Loba

STUART DISCHELL
Dig Safe

STEPHEN DOBYNS
Pallbearers Envying the
*   One Who Rides*
The Porcupine's Kisses

ROGER FANNING
Homesick

AMY GERSTLER
Crown of Weeds
Ghost Girl
Medicine
Nerve Storm

DEBORA GREGER
Desert Fathers, Uranium
*   Daughters*
God

ROBERT HUNTER
Sentinel

BARBARA JORDAN
Trace Elements

MARY KARR
Viper Rum

JACK KEROUAC
Book of Blues
Book of Haikus

JOANNE KYGER
As Ever

ANN LAUTERBACH
If in Time
On a Stair

PHYLLIS LEVIN
Mercury

WILLIAM LOGAN
Macbeth in Venice
Night Battle
Vain Empires

DEREK MAHON
Selected Poems

MICHAEL McCLURE
Huge Dreams: San
*   Francisco and Beat*
*   Poems*

CAROL MUSKE
An Octave Above Thunder

ALICE NOTLEY
The Descent of Alette
Disobedience
Mysteries of Small Houses

LAWRENCE RAAB
The Probable World
Visible Signs

STEPHANIE STRICKLAND
V

ANNE WALDMAN
Kill or Cure
Marriage: A Sentence

PHILIP WHALEN
Overtime: Selected Poems

ROBERT WRIGLEY
Lives of the Animals
Reign of Snakes

JOHN YAU
Borrowed Love Poems

P.O. 0003361212